Hurricane Sisters

Hurricane Sisters

Poems by
Ginger Andrews

Story Line Press
Ashland, Oregon

For Mary Beth, Donna June, BobEtta,
& for Gary Lee

© 2004 by Ginger Andrews
First Printing

Published by Story Line Press
Three Oaks Farm
PO Box 1240, Ashland, Oregon 97520-0055
www.storylinepress.com

This publication was made possible thanks in part to the
generous support of our individual contributors.

Cover art by Carol Vernon
Book design by Sharon McCann

—

Library of Congress Cataloging-in-Publication Data

Andrews, Ginger, 1956-
Hurricane sisters : poems / by Ginger Andrews.
p. cm.
ISBN 1-58654-037-8
I. Title.
PS3551.N4177H87 2004
811'.54—dc22
2004000077

Contents

"Somehow it was always raining
behind the eyes of Oregon girls."
—Nelson Algren, *A Walk on the Wild Side*

"If our hearts do not condemn us, we have confidence before God,
and receive from him anything we ask."
—I John 3:21

Acknowledgments

The author gratefully acknowledges the editors of the following publications in which these poems appeared, sometimes in different versions:

Emerging Infectious Diseases: "Divine Mathematics"
The Hudson Review: "The Cure," "Neon," "Primping in the Rearview Mirror," "Real Men," and "Yes"
MARGIE: "What a Homeless Man Wants," "I am 45 Today," "Old Cleaning Ladies," and "Prayer, One"
Ship of Fools: "Mary Kay"

With love and gratitude to my sisters and my brother; and to Mikey, "Catfish" Dave, Josephine Bridges, Charles Goodrich, Douglas Goetsch, Robert McDowell, Robert Cohen, Paula Dietz, Jay Schroder, Joseph Millar, Dorianne Laux, and the late, great Ann Silsbee. Thanks to the Wednesday night ladies Bible class, and to Garrison Keillor for reading "The Cure," "The Way Things are in Eastside," "Divine Mathematics," and "After Church" on The Writer's Almanac radio program. Very special thanks to Laura B. Sillerman, who knows how much I love my sisters, and understands the importance of buying new shoes. Her kindness and support mean more than I can say.

Introduction

The Poetry of Ginger Andrews

I MET GINGER ANDREWS for the first time at Oregon's Coos Bay Writers Conference in 1997, where I taught a poetry workshop in which she was an occasional participant. There was a good reason for her sporadic attendance, which we discussed before the workshop's first session. Ginger explained that she was short on cash, but had worked out a trade with the conference's director, the poet Mary Scheirman. She would be able to attend some of the conference in exchange for housecleaning work.

In fact, housecleaning was, and is, her profession. With her sisters, she has for many years supported herself in this way. It is not the poet's vocation we most easily imagine. Ginger does not have an M.F.A. in writing; she did not attend college. She married young, had two sons, divorced, and remarried. She has never taught for a living.

In my workshop in Coos Bay, Ginger rarely spoke. But it was obvious that she was wide open and tuned in to every word, to every concept discussed. She observed, she witnessed with extraordinary focus. When she did speak, the other participants paid attention with a respect and concentration that does not always bless a writing workshop. Without saying so, every participant in the room got the fact that when Ginger had something to say, it would be wise to listen carefully.

When poems of hers finally appeared on our worksheet, I believe our group was unanimous in its realization that her talent stood somehow apart. I recall the occasions in my experience when I felt the same: In the early seventies when I was a student of Raymond Carver's and discovered his stories and poems; when I met Mark Jarman in George Hitchcock's writing workshop in 1972; reading the poems of Rusty White, a student in several workshops I taught in Indiana, and later, discovering the poetry of David Mason, Amy Uyematsu, and the late Irish poet, Noelle Vial.

I've had the good fortune to read, and in many cases publish, thousands of extraordinary poems. But every so often, one meets a poetry that is so individual in character and execution it almost seems to exist outside its time. Of course, that is illusion. Such poetry is more of its time than all the rest. Perhaps the poet's unstinting vision startles us, making us aware of the hard, clear light surrounding us.

One notices early, in meeting Ginger Andrews for the first time, her calm center. A religious person (she also teaches Sunday school), Ginger emanates a compassionate, generous radiance. In her poems, letters, and speech, she seems wise beyond her time. It should not surprise us, then, to discover that humility is a primary characteristic of her life and work.

Humility is not often attributed to poets, but in Ginger Andrews it is genuine. She is self-effacing to the point of consistently devaluing her own poetry. She is shy. Even today, she becomes almost physically ill before giving a reading or meeting with a class. Yet she is so good on the platform—and I have seen this on several occasions—audiences literally do not want to let her go at program's end. This is true whether she is reading to a packed bookstore in Ashland, Oregon, or talking to a large audience of teachers and fellow writers at the Associated Writing Programs convention in Palm Springs. Ginger cares so much about people, all people. Her audiences get that. I believe that she becomes, in their eyes, a daughter, mother, best friend, sister, lover, wife, or teacher. It's comforting just to be in her company. She has the gift of feeling familiar.

Ginger's calm, compassion, generosity, vulnerability, humility, and one trait I have not yet mentioned, a perfectly pitched sense of humor, combine to make her poetry unique. It misses something to describe Ginger's verse as Realism, though it is that, or an example of the *Just Plain Folks* school of poetry. To say these things and leave it at that is to miss everything.

Ginger's poetry invites readers in. It is direct and surprising in its ability to hold a reader's attention. Like the prose styles of Ernest Hemingway or Raymond Carver, or the poetry of Robert Creeley or William Carlos Williams, it all looks so simple. Until one tries to do it.

A lot of the poetry written in any age seems to have little to do with the life of that age. A poet's creative drive originates in a deeply internalized place. Many poets find that place but cannot resurface to connect with others, with us. Time remembers best the few poets who do.

One cannot doubt that Ginger Andrews has traveled far through her familiar history, and made it all the way back to a reader who forever asks, "What have you got to tell me?" Before long, that reader feels as if she is hearing her own story, and making valuable discoveries that had never been hers before.

In a class conscious culture, it is the rare individual whose life example and life's work erases class barriers. Abraham Lincoln and Martin Luther King possessed this gift. Walt Whitman had it. Ginger Andrews has it, too. It's likely that her ability to identify with everyone, and to observe with tenderness everything that happens, prompted Garrison Keillor to read poems from her first book, *An Honest Answer*, on National Public Radio's *The Writer's Almanac* no less than eighteen times. Mr. Keillor, who is himself profoundly successful in bringing people together, surely sees in Ginger Andrews a kindred spirit.

Many of her poems begin with the most down-to-earth settings and situations. A woman's bursitis eases up, allowing her to sleep again on her afflicted shoulder; another buys Mary Kay products from a "young girl"; a third wakes up wrestling with "the ache and shame / of the dream of the man / old enough to be your father, / caressing the back of your neck..."; a sister confesses her love of Ramen noodles; another calls up "her old walking pharmaceutical of a friend" to ask about the spelling of a drug that begins with the letter M; a woman scrubs a bath tub at her first housecleaning job of the day; a beautiful morning breaks through valley fog. Modest beginnings, yes, but looking at the way these poems develop provides useful insights into the poet's intuitive and practical strategies.

The bursitis poem chronicles the daily physical tasks the relieved woman can now accomplish ("You can button your pants, hook your bra, / tie your shoes, shower and shave / under both arms..."). The poem turns on lines of unexpected exuberance: "You can just stand around flapping / your arms like an idiot, or an angel." These signature lines carry important insight. A Ginger Andrews' strength is to see with compassion the idiot and the angel as one being. From that turning point, the poem blossoms. The speaker imagines thanking God "for the new old you," imagines setting new goals, committing, and confessing sins. She imagines helping others, and in doing so, changing her whole life, *if she wants to.*

That closing qualifier, for seasoned readers of Andrews' poems, is rejuvenating and familiar. Time and again, she reminds us that one must be responsible, must lift the weight and bear it, must want to do a thing before the thing can be done. In doing this, she undercuts potential sentimentality that would make the poem pleasant fare, but less startling, less memorable.

In the Mary Kay poem, the narrator wants to help a "young gal / who's down on her luck." But in the poem's turning point, she realizes that she wants "at least one of each item / on every page, just go nuts..." Suddenly, a small domestic poem becomes a snapshot of greed, our national obsession with consuming. It cries out the complexity of wanting, always wanting what we don't or can't have.

This revelation also surfaces in the poem about the sex dream, which is not simply lurid. In an Andrews poem, the obvious is never the point. In fact, the poem explores "the sorrow / that mixes death and sex."

In another poem, the sister praising Ramen noodles lists the things she must do without because she is poor: "No washing whites in hot. / No deodorant, floss, Q-tips, Kotex or Midol. / One-ply toilet paper. No Kleenex. No cotton balls. / No new shoes. No espresso. No Red Bulls or Taco Bell. / No vacation, Lord knows, and no cash for the collection plate." Who cannot be moved by this list of things so many of us take for granted and cannot imagine being refused? If the poem ended there it would be powerful, but only as an indictment of poverty and systems that perpetuate it. Andrews takes the poem one step further, transforming the societal problem into a human problem. After her list the woman concludes, "I can take on more cleaning jobs. I can do that." The defiant yet matter of fact "I can do that" brings all our attention back to the human being, the enduring and triumphant individual face indicting a national stigma.

The poem beginning with a sister's call to a friend about a particular drug is not as serious or grim as others. Often, one meets an element of humor in an Andrews poem, and occasionally a poem dominated by it. This particular poem evolves into a playful romp through the way we pronounce and mispronounce words and the comical consequences that attend such moments. It reminds us that laughter comforts our ever attending sense of desolation.

The housecleaning poem is bold and marvelous. The narrator, upstairs scrubbing the tub, breaks into "Old MacDonald Had a Farm, starting with the *E I E I O...*" Two sisters downstairs, one cleaning an oven, the other dusting blinds, and a third in the basement, also scouring a tub, all join in "on the *moo-moos here, moo-moos there*." Upstairs, the narrator, her lungs filling with the fumes of cleaning products, begins "hacking on the *quack-quacks*." The oven cleaning sister, "now singing along, says, Hey, are you all right up there?" So the poem ends. Direct and simple. Yet as each sister is introduced, in an appropriate economy of line and image, we learn a lot about each one's health and money woes. Because we do know, when we come to and experience that last question—"Hey, are you all right up there?"—we feel its depth, its urgency, its pathos. We comprehend the sisters' vulnerability. The moments of working together, even on a tough job, are precious. It is a beautiful and uplifting Sisterhood poem.

Finally, in the poem beginning on a lovely day, we experience a rapid transformation as we accompany the narrator inside a courtroom where her hard-luck brother is sentenced to ten days in jail, thirty months probation, and a fifteen hundred-dollar fine. As he is led away in handcuffs, the narrator muses on the legal system's harshness against a man "whose last arrest was six long years ago, / after our father, and then our sister died," and she thinks about his children "who're used to their dad serving them / hot oatmeal and buttered toast / every morning before school." As he is led away with his fellow inmates "down the long hall," we feel with a poignant thud how far, in just twenty-six lines, we have come from that beautiful morning where we started.

Don't we all yearn for poems and stories that sweep us up in their arms and deliver us? But deliver us from, and deliver us to, what? From evil, of course; or to an understanding of evil; from loneliness and despair to love and exultation; from suspicion and bitterness to trust and compassion; from emptiness to belief, to faith; from isolation to community. In poem after poem, and I hope in many books to come, Ginger Andrews flawlessly delivers us. She is an American treasure, wholly formed, who we are just beginning to discover. How fortunate to be living now, if only for that.

Robert McDowell
Ashland, Oregon

I

The Hurricane Sisters Work Regardless

Scrubbing the upstairs tub at our first housecleaning job of the day,
I hate to whine about some trivial fever, chills and sore throat. Instead,
I decide to sing Old MacDonald Had a Farm, starting with the *E I E I O*,
to my oven-cleaning downstairs sister who has a large uterine tumor
and knows it won't get removed unless it becomes absolutely necessary.
She doesn't have insurance, and free clinic patients have to make do
with whatever surgeon volunteers, whenever there's time.

My diabetic sister, who hasn't had a slice of pie, a doughnut
or a cigarette in years, who watched me hog down half a bag
of miniature Snickers on the way to work, and might not believe
I could eat like that with a fever, who is dusting mini blinds
on the middle-floor windows, while ignoring the nasty body aches
resulting from Wednesday's flu shot, joins in on the *moo-moo's here,
moo-moo's there.*

Also scrubbing a tub, my basement sister, who's on her second round
of antibiotics for her third sinus infection of the year, hollers
up the stairway, *here a moo, there a moo.*

My lungs full of Lysol Basin Tub & Tile cleaner, I'm hacking
on the *quack-quacks* when my oven-cleaning sister,
now singing along, says, Hey, are you all right up there?

3

Sugar Tit

Near death, high on morphine, Dad reminisces.
Me and your mother were lucky. Six healthy kids.
'Course, we almost lost you to pneumonia, thanks to
that stupid ass Dr. Black. *Just take her home,* he said,
there's nothing we can do for her.

We'd have lost your sister too, if it weren't for that old lady
Beatrice stopping by. She said to your mother, *Almeda,*
this baby's starvin' to death. Your milk's bad, honey.
She put a clump of sugar in the corner of a tobacco sack,
added a little water, gave it to your sister to suck,
then had me run to get two cans of Carnation.

Lifting his hands, Dad spreads his fingers as wide as he can.
Your mother had all kinds of milk, he says. She was just so full
of milk. Dad puts his hands together, slowly lets them fall.

Momma

Oh my big, tall, gray-haired Momma
with holes cut in the sides of her shoes
so her hard yellow corns wouldn't get pinched,
wearing the same thin dress and apron
she wore the day before,
her wide shoulders, her hips like a breadbox
looming above me as she stood
a little bent over at the kitchen sink
scrubbing the big blue stew pot
as I sat on the cold linoleum floor beneath her
playing with metal measuring spoons
and an empty Lipton tea box, listening
to her soft voice singing *Allegheny Moon*.

Real Men

work at the sawmill and
refuse to eat bologna sandwiches.
They like leftover meatloaf or tuna
—if it's not that damn grated crap
with damn ground bones in it.
They work lots of Saturdays,
pay for groceries with cash,
wait in their cars while their wives
shop with one baby on their hip,
one in the cart, one at their feet,
and one on the way.
They have garages they built themselves
with really big vices on the end
of a workbench, and hundreds
of Gerber baby food jars full
of nuts and bolts and screws
that are screwed into the lids
that are nailed to the ceiling
by the light bulb that hangs
in front of the calendar
with pictures of fancy cars
with shiny bumpers
and women with long legs
and low-cut summer tops
and red lipstick and high heels.
They will give you a nickel
for penny candy
if you get in their way.
They say Jesus Christ a lot.

They don't like preachers, but
they are happy to drive you
to church on Sundays,
drop you off and pick you up
at twelve o'clock sharp.

Foreplay

Sometimes that one fat piece
of bread gets hung up in your toaster
but—because you're scrambling around,
dumping coffee grounds, refilling the pot,
closing the refrigerator with one toe
as you're talking on the phone
to some kind blind man selling light bulbs,
your head bent to your shoulder,
holding the phone in place,
pinching the tender skin of your collar bone
where your nightshirt has slipped,
your old fat cat under your feet meowing like a sick calf—
you are unaware of the bread's thickness,
till smoke gets in your eyes and nostrils,
as your back is turned,
as you're opening the silverware drawer,
feeling around for the butter knife,
which must be in the dirty dishwater,
and you say, Damn.
The poor man on the phone
thinks you're not even listening.
You say you're sorry you're not interested,
as you butter the burnt slices,
give one to your husband who eats anything.

Washing Her Feet

If in the middle of your blessed camping trip
that you couldn't afford to begin with,
your favorite Uncle dies and you get that raw
burning throat with one of those horrible headaches
from trying not to cry at his memorial service
where you smell like camp smoke and have gas
from pork & beans, where your poorest sister
comes right out and asks if maybe you could pay
her seven-dollar-a-night extra vehicle fee
if she spends what money she does have on food
because she just really needs to get away,
and you know that you won't have time alone
with the stars and God like you dreamed of,
you say, You bet. No problem. Then later,
when your eleven-year-old ratty-haired niece with a head cold
asks if you would heat her up some water
to mix with the cold from the campsite spigot
so she can soak her dirty feet, when you've just
spent half the morning cooking and cleaning,
and have camp grit between your own toes,
and suddenly feel very much like crying
the cry you didn't cry the day before,
you suck it up again and say, Sure, Sweetie,
giving her that last, white, clean washrag
you'd saved to wash your face.

Neon

A little depressed
on a cold, gray, rainy day
sitting at the Star Mart drive-up window
in my (you guessed it) gray car
waiting on a twenty-ounce mocha
staring out my window through rain
while rain soaks the sleeve of my sweatshirt
because I've left my window down and
I'm thinking I should roll it up but
that if I do the girl will motion
for me to roll it back down again. Lord,
when did life in this jerk-water town
shut down anyway?
The bay behind the bare alder trees,
the sky, the pavement, all gray.
Across the street, the parking lot at Gino's Pizza
is empty, their sign burnt out
all except for one big bright neon Z.

The Cure

Lying around all day
with some strange new deep blue
weekend funk, I'm not really asleep
when my sister calls
to say she's just hung up
from talking with Aunt Bertha
who is 89 and ill but managing
to take care of Uncle Frank
who is completely bed ridden.
Aunt Bert says
it's snowing there in Arkansas,
on Catfish Lane, and she hasn't been
able to walk out to their mailbox.
She's been suffering
from a bad case of the mulleygrubs.
The cure for the mulleygrubs,
she tells my sister,
is to get up and bake a cake.
If that doesn't do it, put on a red dress.

Last Sunday

I went to visit my alcoholic brother
who took me for a walk on a red road with his black lab
who couldn't wait to jump in the levee
where he stirred up an albino muskrat—
beautiful and strange. I had an out-of-body experience
as the muskrat slipped away, as the dog looked back up
at my sober brother whose gray hair was suddenly white,
flowing in the lukewarm breeze, as he stood tall
on the grassy bank, as the sun shot through the overcast sky,
as sweat beads trickled down my temples.

We had walked much farther than I'd realized.
I was wearing new shoes, got a blister on my heel.
About sundown we drank Sam's Choice colas.
My brother found three bags of chips in his cupboard.
Ridges, Sour Cream & Onion, or Bar-B-Q, he said.
He made me a bologna sandwich that tasted like heaven.

What Our Family Needs

My thirteen-year-old niece
is living with my stay-at-home brother
and his significant other, who is working
at the register behind the counter at Goodwill, laughing
at the too short, too tight, and way too low-cut blouses
my niece has chosen off the New Arrivals rack.

She's trying to teach my niece, who is grounded
for thirty days, and got to come to the store
only because I'm visiting from out of town,
that what our family needs is a nerd.
Just a nice, quiet guy who gets good grades,
like that sweet boy who offers to carry her books home.
Forget about those shifty-eyed, lean-bodied skaters
who smoke pot and do Ecstasy.
Listen to me, Honey, she says,
you've got to get yourself a geek.

Angelica

My nephew's newest girlfriend
is beautiful, shy, nervous, silent,
until our smart, old, toothless cat
jumps onto her lap to groan
and slobber all over her black Levi's.
Her eyes light up as she scratches
behind Tigger's ears.

When we lived out in the boondocks,
she says, we had three dogs,
three cats,
two gay hamsters,
four rats,
two ferrets,
and one hedgehog named Pinhead
whose cage I had to clean every week
wearing kitchen mitts.
He'd roll up in a ball,
stick out his little deadly spikes,
and hiccup.

My Sister Bob

goes on and on
on the phone
about some decorating tip
she's picked up on HGTV,
how to make your living room look bigger
without knocking out a wall or some such thing,
when she hears me start to breathe
hard and fast and heavy.
She asks if I'm all right.
I say, No. I'm not.
This phone is pinching the crap
out of my ear and shoulder
while I'm trying to listen to you
and cram Mikey's big fat
Italian roast beef sandwich
into this stupid itsy Ziploc bag—
but it just won't zip!
Bob says, Why don't you just take a bite out of it?

Possum Poop

My sister Donna June calls my sister Mary Beth
to tell her I called Mikey home from work
in the middle of his swing shift
to get a possum out of the bedroom
where it's peed and left a pile
stinking to high heaven.
Mary Beth calls our sister Bob
who calls me after she's called the Carpet Hut people
who tell her that short of buying new carpet—
they're having a Spring Sale this month—
I should try club soda, not 7-Up, not ginger ale.
Pour some over the soiled area. Let it dry completely,
then vacuum.

Friday Night

Exhausted after a particularly long week
of cleaning houses, we decide to get fast food
at a drive-up. My sister orders
two crunchy tacos and a small Pepsi.
The young voice from the speaker asks, Would you
like to add an Oreo Brownie for dessert today,
for just 99 cents? My sister says, You know what,
I'm gonna say yes this time, because I've said no
soooooo many times before.

Space # 22
for Everett Richardson

I tell myself I couldn't be happier,
sitting here at my warped camp trailer table
with bags under my eyes, frizzy hair, no makeup,
and the lower backache you're guaranteed to wake up with
from sleeping in the pull-out bed.
I'm sipping scalding hot percolated coffee
from a *Jesus, The Gift of Hope* ceramic mug I'd forgotten about.
You know, reject cups, old stained Tupperware bowls, the odd
non-matching forks, spoons and the like, that end up in your camper.
Not that I've rejected Jesus, but God knows I needed to get away
from my cleaning jobs. Every day, scrubbing, mopping, ironing, reaching
for possible cobwebs in the corners of all those gorgeous skylights
in darn near every room of every house I've cleaned with my sisters
these last fifteen years. I don't want to clean anymore.
I'm tired of Windex. I'm tired of people. I'm tired of sisters,
nieces, nephews, my daughter, my son, my other son and his wife,
all my friends, my sweet, smiling-over-the-fence, near-death neighbor
who stopped smiling long enough to look lost
when he told me the doctors want to cut on him some more.Yeah, he said,
it's like the Grim Reaper's following me around all the time.
He asked if I was going to write another poem about him.
I told him I would.

I love him and everybody else I got away from
to be alone in this not-so-far-from-home campsite, sitting here tilted,
one end of the camper obviously too high.
The indoor-outdoor carpet damp under my feet—
the water storage tank filled a little too full by my husband
who got me here, set me up, and promised to return
with campfire wood. My socks are wet.
After days of perfect July sun, we've hit a cold snap.
It's raining here in space # 22.
The drops from trees overhead sound like little bombs
bursting in the silence as I sit here freezing my butt off,
wondering which cubbyhole I put the Mixed Berry Granola Bars in.
I blow steam off my Yuban with blue lips, my cold hands cupping
the hot, forgotten Jesus cup.

II

Bad To The Bone

It's not like you wake up one morning
forty-five, depressed and clueless, sorry
for eating that second slice of pie,
for the prayer you didn't pray
because you fell asleep in your recliner
watching Law & Order Special Victims Unit,
a rerun, three women raped by the same man,
surprised in their beds, asleep,
some wacko with a stocking pulled over his face
and a can of mace, your husband stoking the fire
because you said you were cold. You wake up
with your mouth open, dried out, your tongue
swollen, the ceiling fan whirring directly above you,
the house dark, your shirt twisted, your mind
slowly untangling as you remember
your 7:45 AM dental appointment
just as George Thorogood
begins yelling *On The Day I Was Born*
from your radio alarm clock down the hall
where your husband is out like a light,
oblivious to the thrill.

Primping in the Rearview Mirror

after a solid ten-minute bout of tears,
hoping that the Safeway man who stocks the shelves
and talked to you once for thirty minutes about specialty jams,
won't ask if you're all right, or tell you you look like shit
and then have to apologize as he remembers that you don't
like cuss words and you don't date ex prison guards
because you're married. The truth is you're afraid
this blue-eyed charismatic sexist hunk of a reject just might
trigger another round of tears, that you'll lean into him
right in front of the eggs and milk, crying like a baby,
your face buried in his chest just below the two opened
buttons of his tight white knit shirt, his big cold hands
pressed to the small of your back, pulling you closer
to whisper that everything will be all right.

Crazy

The lead guitar player and singer
in my husband's high school rock band
once told me when I was singing
along with the radio to Patsy Cline—
I'm crazy for tryin', I'm crazy for cryin',
and I'm crazy for lovin' you—
that I sounded exactly like her.
I said, I wish! But I was lying,
thinking he was exactly right.
He insisted I really should be in the band.
I said, Oh my goodness, no.
Just eighteen, with a baby
on my lap, and one in my belly,
I said, No thanks, Jim.
But I remember my heart turning over,
skipping a couple of beats,
as I leaned into him on that long, tight corner,
as I sat in the middle of our truck seat,
on that hot summer Saturday afternoon,
as if I were free to fall.

5:01 AM

There is the ache and shame
of the dream of the man
old enough to be your father,
caressing the back of your neck,
then the length of your spine
all the way down, the lower
stomach pressure, fullness,
a need to pee
no matter the clock's red glow, that flash
of God, of lightning on headstones,
having sex in a hospital bed?
Thoughts of that first drag
of a cigarette, the sorrow
that mixes death and sex. Oh—
that movie last night—that woman
telling the man whose true love
is trapped on some island with Harrison Ford,
presumed dead, that *Everybody knows you have sex
when somebody dies.* Of course
the man's fiancée isn't really dead. Anyway,
Harrison is not old enough to be your father,
doesn't look anything like the prune-skinned creep
who turned you on last night.

South of Salina

Maybe it was the Ben Affleck Sandra Bullock movie
we woke up to at the Vagabond Motel and Restaurant,
or the old chubby waitress who wagged an arthritic finger
and said, No, no, Sweetie. It's 10 AM, not 8 AM.
Maybe it was you, back behind the wheel on Interstate 70,
spilling V8 Splash on your genuine Jet Pilot T-shirt,
or me finding my hot pink Pilot V-Ball roller pen in the bottom
of my new purple travel purse, its ink leaked out all over, and me
trying to write poetry with bright pink stains on my fingers.
Maybe it's the way we're sharing the one Kleenex.
Oh! This hot-pink ink and orange Splash sticky stuff everywhere...500 miles
from Arkansas and in-laws, chiggers and ticks, humidity,
sweet iced tea, biscuits and gravy, hashbrowns, collard greens,
thunderstorms and lightning bugs—God knows I love the little glowers.
Right now I feel much better about Hays Kansas
than I did that first time driving through, wondering
why God made Kansas. Smelly, hot, flat, hazy, endless.
And if you weren't fidgeting with the cruise control,
frowning over road construction and the V8 stain—
looks like some got on your button fly—
I'd ask if we could just up and move here, live the rest of our lives
as wheat or pig farmers. You know, live a quiet life right here
somewhere south of Salina. But you'd think I was kidding,
maybe ask if I'd left my thinker in the toilet—a new expression for you,
one that made us both bust up somewhere back near Winnemucca.

Somewhere in Idaho

driving into a blinding sunset
you offer me the shirt off your back
to blow my nose on
because you're feeling guilty
for having left me
in the sweltering heat of the car
when you stopped
in whatever jerk-water tumbleweed hotter-than-hell town
to look for some all-important chrome piece
for your precious '67 Malibu
that I encouraged you to buy before we left on vacation,
instead of the new linoleum for the kitchen
I've been wanting for years now,
and because you forgot to get napkins at McDonald's
like I asked you to when I gave you two dollars
to buy me one of those new fruit and yogurt parfaits.
I know you're stressed out about all the money
we've spent on this two-week trip to Arkansas
to help your parents move,
how we've spent as much coming as going,
how much more gas it takes with the air conditioning on,
how it surges and screws up the engine in our gutless four-banger,
so I say, Just shut it off, and never mind about me blowing my nose.

Near Hays, Kansas

on her way home from Arkansas,
a cleaning lady in a tank top
and baggy shorts
is sitting in the passenger's seat
of her economy Nissan.
Her husband is driving, smoking
a cigarette and singing
along with the radio to Jim Morrison:
Well I woke up this morning
and I got myself a beer...
They are in the fast lane
about to pass a car with Kansas plates
when she props her elbow
on the window's ledge, tucks
her fingers around the little gutter
of the car top, and flexes her bicep.
She knows it looks
like some weightlifter-chick's bicep,
but she's just working class,
got her muscles from scrubbing and waxing,
and she knows that she's striking a pose, maybe
because the scenery is boring,
or because she's just so hot! It's so sultry and sticky,
and she can't believe she found a tick on her tit
and a chigger in her armpit *after*
her motel shower in Silverthorne, Colorado,
and she's itching all over, has a little headache,
and a long way to go. And she's maybe hoping
that whoever's in the car they're passing

looks over and sees her kind of sexy, muscley arm,
and thinks it's a good-looking arm.
Or maybe they'll happen to notice
the out of state license plates and think,
Wow. Oregon.

A Hundred Miles from Gallup

I look up from my cheap romance novel,
cruising west on I-40,
the sinking New Mexico sun in my eyes,
Little River Band *Reminiscing* on the radio
on our way home to Oregon
when just like that I'm in love
with Albuquerque:
the pretty yellow bug guts on the windshield,
the funky self-inflicted tattoo of your old girlfriend
on your forearm, the way your eyes are glazed,
glued to the highway, your right foot relaxed,
the cruise control set on 80,
the cute red heart on the half cup
of cold Love's Truck Stop coffee
in the pull-out drink holder between us.
We've got Moon Pies, Mountain Dew,
orange juice and string cheese in the cooler,
a bag of pretzels under my seat.
For the first time in fourteen years of marriage,
you have heartburn. It must be all that cinnamon
in the homemade zucchini bread Maw baked us
for the trip home. I find two Tums
in the lint at the bottom of my purse.
I'm brushing Moon Pie crumbs off my lap
when the sexy-voiced deejay says, of all things,
Be careful, ladies, sugar makes your butt fat. I flip
my seat back, close my eyes. You say, You know,
we're only about a hundred miles from Gallup
and a cheap motel.

Weatherman

He flicks his wrist toward
the highs and lows
up and down the coast,
tapping a finger inland
to Klamath Falls
where it's freezing
in spite of spring.
There's a dab of Grey Poupon
on my index finger,
the smell of sliced onion
trapped in my adenoids.
If only you would get your own self up
and off to work, pack your own lunch,
pour your own coffee, leave me
free to write before I'm scrambled
like the eggs I offer
as you listen to the sports report,
jazzed over the Trailblazers win,
scratching behind our fat cat's ears.
We've got tree people protesting
a private landowner
who's bulldozed his own trees down,
a spokesperson for the pope, who says,
he will deal with all that sex mess,
Bin Laden looking sickly,
something about stem cells
and Parkinson's disease.
Your work shirt has a missing button.

My sister's in the middle of her fourth divorce.
Our neighbor is undergoing a quadruple bypass.
With a Cheshire grin,
the weatherman predicts sun.
He has nice white teeth,
a skinny neck, a bright red tie.

Divine Mathematics

In her second month of a three-month-long virus,
which, according to half a dozen fellow victims,
does not respond to antibiotics, my sister apologizes
for needing to take her third nap of the day
on my sofa. Homeless and divorced, she's relieved
to know that a trip to the doctor most likely wouldn't
do her any good, especially since she has no insurance
coverage of any kind, except on her '78 Ford Fairmont,
with its brand new master cylinder, which thanks to God
and Les Schwab's low monthly payment plan,
should be paid for by the end of the year,
at which time she hopes to get a rotation,
two new tires, and a badly needed front end alignment,
all for just under a hundred bucks.

How to Write a Poem

It helps if you drink
espresso, take B vitamins,
and believe in God.
Live in a small mill town.
Marry a man with a big heart,
a big truck, a strong back,
and a chainsaw.
Have four children,
one bathroom,
and wood heat.
Chop kindling.
Love rain.
Eat meatloaf.
Call your sisters every day.
Listen, at least once,
to an all-black congregation
singing *I'll fly Away.*
Live by the sea.
Love those who curse you.
Read Ecclesiastes and Billy Collins.
Attend writers' workshops
if they're catered.
Vacation only in Arkansas.

What I Know about Birds

My mother was a Byrd before she married
my father and became a Dearstine.
She had bird legs—long and skinny.
I have them, too, only mine aren't so long.
And skinny ankles, which are better
than fat ankles on skinny legs.
Playing in the woods once, I found
a bird's nest with little speckled eggs.
My brother told me they belonged to a robin.
I sometimes feed French-fries to the crows
that land in my front yard. Through the years,
I've had hummingbird feeders, and often
stood breathless, listening
to the whirring of their tiny wings.
Once I bought a book on Birds of the Pacific
Northwest, but I lost it.

Word Association

My sister calls up her old walking pharmaceutical of a friend
to ask if she knows the spelling of the drug that starts with a M,
and sounds something like Mad Vick. Her doctor's just
prescribed it as a preventative high blood pressure treatment
for diabetics, and she wants to look it up on the Internet.
Oh yeah, her friend says, it's called Mavik. I've been taking it for years.
The way I remembered how to say it, is that it sounded a lot like
my old Maverick car, but without the R. Got it! my sister says.
Word association. Works every time. Which reminds me
of the time my ex, Travis, was doing something in the kitchen,
and heard someone on TV say, *Tavis.* He said it sounded like
someone was trying to say his name, but didn't know how.
I wonder, my sister says, what it would sound like
to leave the R out of every R word? I guess I'd be Ms. Dea-stine,
living off Boadway on Eveett Steet.

Poetry

After fifteen years of marriage,
you'd think you would know
what thrills me, I say,
as we pass a Barnes & Noble.
If you want me to pretend
that I'm half as jazzed to look
at the new Dodge Dakota
as I am to finger the spines
of new poetry, fine. Let's talk V-6
versus V-8, let's talk extended cab,
dual carbs, lift kits, the slotted
versus the honeycomb grill.
Let's talk 4X4, off road,
cruise control, traction,
chrome and color options—
black, white, the new deep blue.
You ask me if I want you
to turn around. I say, No.

Communication

I refuse to come right out and tell you
that I feel old, unattractive, unappreciated,
and flat-out taken advantage of.
Instead, I ask, Do you ever feel
really, really selfish? And you say,
All the time.

Something That Recently Happened

to you or me, or my friend who moved to Russia,
maybe something someone said or read in the paper;
maybe that stress test my oldest sister passed,
or the storm out of nowhere
that snapped our huge Douglas fir in half;
the way it fell east into the empty field
instead of west into our back yard
where it most likely would have landed
slam on top of your shop, crashing through
the metal roof and quite possibly smashing
your three-quarters restored 1967 Malibu Sport Coupe.
But no, it was something else. Maybe the queen-sized
second-hand store bed my sister helped load into the borrowed truck
for her neighbor who's been sleeping on her floor for six months,
the possible mistake of their stopping
at the expensive furniture store on their way home,
where Annette fell in love with this wonderful white wicker rocker,
spending half her next month's rent, actually digging
in the bottom of her purse for change, coming up
a few dollars and cents short, my sister loaning her the difference,
Annette beside herself with gratitude.
I'm not at home when my sister calls, wanting help
with hauling the boxsprings and big fat mattress up the steep stairs.
But I'm thinking it might be that e-mail from my friend
in Russia, who's lately been bothered by someone's grandmother
struggling across an icy street, using a 6 ft. 2X4 as a cane.

The Way Things Are in Eastside

So these two smart, slick dudes from South Africa and Romania
somehow get hold of our credit card number and e address,
charging up hundreds of dollars which screws
our banking and puts a stop to any check writing
on the very evening I'd planned on Chinese take-out.
Just my good fortune, I find a six serving size frozen dinner entrée—
Salisbury steak, wedged behind the ice trays in my freezer—especially
since my favorite nephew happens by, hungry and broke,
and then my sister who's never eaten right, so I
somehow feel blessed anyway, until my husband comes home
frowning, wound tight because he hit a deer on his way to work,
busting up the whole front end of his Nissan—this, just a week after
dropping full coverage because the truck's finally paid off. I tell him to sit, eat,
take my car to the police station to file the computer fraud claim. Speaking
of foreign countries, my nephew says, How are your friends in Russia doing?
He wonders if they might find him a nice Russian gal who'd be willing to come
to Coos County and marry him. My sister almost chokes on her baked potato.
I'm telling you, he says, there ain't no good women left in Eastside, Oregon.

III

Tender

I make friends with whatever insect it is
that looks like a mosquito but isn't. I name him Tender.
My little buddy, unlike a real bloodsucker, wouldn't hurt a flea.
He has a broken leg, which, I tell him, is better
than insulin-dependant diabetes, non-Hodgkin's lymphoma,
a daughter on crack, a niece in detention, or a seventeen-year-old
cat with asthma, a thyroid condition and ear mites.
You are lucky, I say, that old Fat Cat can no longer swat bugs like you
directly into her mouth to chomp and swallow.

Tender lights on the counter next to a dirty spaghetti pan.
I tell him that there are poems under dishwater, especially
after the sun goes down and the water turns cold.
Sucking at soap suds, Tender looks bored. Outside
the kitchen window, the moon eats her own face.

Everyday Sinners

Blessed be the Pop Tart eaters,
the Mountain Dew drinkers,
the smokers, jokers, and self-centered
whiners married to slovenly mates
and old hippies
who haven't been stoned since
Black Sabbath concerts in the 70's,
who hope their children's faith
is in the new Youth Minister
instead of good old Mom or Dad,
who pray for strength and forgiveness
every evening, in their closets, on their knees,
or during pet food commercials with their eyes open,
and their hearts on fire.

How to Ease Suffering
—for Catfish

Tell about the time somebody slipped
blotter acid in your sarsaparilla down in Sausalito
and you made friends with that little blonde-
haired blue-eyed two-year old in a stroller,
who laughed and cooed for what seemed like hours and hours,
till her face melted, and her mother, wearing this tie-dyed tank top
without a bra, slammed her daughter's diaper bag into the side
of your head, the little zipper part puncturing your ear lobe.
Blood ran down your neck. You swiped the trickle with your hand,
licking off the blood which tasted exactly like grape Nehi.
Next thing you remember is peeing on a cactus, then
puking into the bed of some long-haired guy's pickup,
little bubbles popping out your nose. Inside the cab,
the long-haired guy was French kissing some skinny gal
who sat half on his lap, half on the steering wheel.
Giant mosquitoes bounced around the dome light, glowing
and sparkling like orange metalflake, while the Eagles sang
mirrors on the ceiling, pink champagne on ice.

In Times Like These
—September 12

You praise your old feather pillow, even though it's lost its fluff,
causing your head to lie flat, which causes the bursitis in your shoulder
to ache the minute your eyes open.
You are blessed to be a cleaning lady, married to a mill worker,
living the quiet life in small town Oregon.

You get over the fact that you have painted your walls pink.
Wispy Beige *may look off-white on the paint store's color card, but it's not.*
You accept the challenge of working with what you have. And you have
    plenty.

Yesterday you admitted to yourself that you really are in menopause,
but because you moaned about it for years before it actually
    arrived, nobody cares.
So you have a little Buddha belly, bags under your eyes and a mustache.

Today you're giving blood, pasting a little flag in your car window.

Remodeling in December

I find myself teary-eyed over a new vent hose for my dryer.
It's such an inexpensive, important replacement. And it's not that
I'm unappreciative of our brand new almond-tone, elongated Kohler toilet,
replacing the physically challenged one we got free from my nephew, but
there was just something about the way my feet dangled when I sat
on that old throne, how I could click my heels together if I wanted to.
It's just, oh, I don't know, everything—
the old down-on-his-luck family friend & alcoholic we hired,
trying to be nice, save some money, get the master bath remodeled—
at least the toilet flushing, before all the kids come home for Christmas.
Our friend's hands get shaky if he doesn't have a beer before noon.
Like an idiot I run to 7-Eleven to get him a 40-ouncer.
He seems to work best with country music playing.
Turn it up, I say. We warm our backsides by the wood stove,
listening to Vince Gill sing *Blue Christmas.*
A rare snow has fallen.
It's so cold my cats won't go outside,
so icy today, I don't think I'll make it to the store for kitty litter.
We've got this old bottle of Cabernet Sauvignon in the fridge.
It's not beer, but it's here. Our friend apologizes for the sheetrock mess,
that he didn't think to close the bedroom doors.
Hey, my whole house is flocked for the holidays, I say. I like it.
The mail brings a card from my ex-grandma.
In her near-death scrawl she writes:
I know that you will put Christ back into Christmas.

What a Homeless Man Wants

I want new front teeth.

A white T-shirt.

A pair of black Levi's.

Some snakeskin boots.

Oh and the reading glasses I lost last summer
when I fell slam into the river tryin' to fish
and drink and take a leak all at the same time.

And maybe, a woman like you.

I am 45 Today

My father's mother died at 41
in a nuthouse in Branson, Missouri,
beaten to death by fellow inmates
who put bars of soap in socks
and whacked her till her lights went out.
Dad said she made moonshine,
got pregnant during her change-of-life,
lost her mind. His step-Dad and him were scared
she'd burn up the house.
He said they cried on their way
to having her committed.

My mother's mother died at 42
while giving birth to her fourteenth child.

My mother died at 42
of cancer, when I was ten.

My sister died at 44—
cancer.

My nephew calls
to wish me a happy birthday. He swears
I don't look a day over 39.

Working Class, One

A middle-aged cleaning lady
is standing in someone else's beautiful blue kitchen
on the edge of an oval-shaped braided rug
under vaulted ceiling skylights, shaking bagel crumbs
out of a four-slice Cuisinart toaster, then polishing its chrome
with a soft cloth and Windex till it shines like the bumper
of her dead father's 1951 Hudson Hornet.
Maybe this is not a good time to get emotional
over poor dead relations, her pretty mother
who whipped egg whites in a bowl with a fork
until stiff peaks formed, who died
before four-slice toasters were invented,
not that she'd have spent money on any such fancy,
with six kids to feed and a husband
who needed a big car to get them all down the road to Arkansas
to visit the relatives who weren't fortunate enough to move to Oregon
and get good-paying mill jobs, the kinfolk left behind
in the cotton fields back home.

Working Class, Two

She used to muck out rentals
that scatterbrained addicts left
littered with needles, beer bottles,
stinky ashtrays, broken toys,
busted stereos, moldy Tupperware,
filthy clothes and condoms
tied off and tossed in a corner.
Now she works for rich retired people,

some of whom serve her
fresh-ground coffee and homemade cinnamon rolls—
the mouth-watering aromas drifting
through their beautiful three-story homes,
all the way down to the bottom floor where she irons
Van Huesen shirts and Liz Claiborne blouses
with a top-of-the-line Rowenta
while listening to Wagner overtures.

Steamboat

We're sitting around my kitchen table eating egg salad
sandwiches between cleaning jobs,
talking about taking on more.
Don't you think, I say, we should get rid of some,
now that we're old and sick half the time?
You're the one who's always sick, Mary Beth says.
That's right, I say, I'm so sick right now I could throw up.
Be quiet, Donna June says, my soap is on.
Speaking of poetry, I say, not that we were,
I have great news! Garrison Keillor's gonna read
another one of my poems on his radio program!
That's so exciting, BobEtta says. We are *very* proud of you.
Pass the Cheetos. Wiping some egg salad off her chin,
she wonders if I knew that Dad was a poet.
Dad? Stubborn, mean, funny old Dad?
I can see him now, I say, sitting
at his rickety, stained kitchen table, drinking
stale, weak coffee through a straw,
eating Vienna sausage straight from the can,
with those *un*salted Saltines, reading the *National Enquirer.*
Yeah, says Mary Beth. I asked him once if he understood
all those big words he was reading. He said, Nope.
But when he'd come to a word he didn't understand,
he'd just call it STEAMBOAT—and keep right on reading!
Well all I know, BobEtta says, is what he wrote
in my High School annual: *You are my bright and shining star.*
Love, Dad.

Getting Ready to be Poor

My sister laughs, says she can eat Ramen noodles
for lunch and dinner, instead of just for lunch.
It's no big deal, she's been poor before.

No washing whites in hot.
No deodorant, floss, Q-Tips, Kotex or Midol.
One-ply toilet paper. No Kleenex. No cotton balls.

No new shoes. No espresso. No Red Bulls, or Taco Bell.
No vacation, Lord knows, and no cash for the collection plate.
But, she says, I can take on more cleaning jobs. I can do that.

Mary Kay

So you spend almost sixty bucks
to help out some young gal
who's down on her luck,
more than likely high,
as she fills out your order form
for cleanser, toner,
and some under eye night cream
you can't wait to try.
Suddenly
you realize how much
you'd like to order at least one
of each item on every page.
Just go nuts
on shadow, blush,
concealer, candles,
shower gel, foot balm,
Dietary Supplements,
the entire Customized
Skin Care Package
on pages 16, 18, and 25,
the pretty and practical
hot-pink Beaded Lipstick Case—
with mirror!
The Twinkle Twinkle You're A Star
Shimmery Powder in a Puff
Limited Edition Gift Set,

the Favorite Things
Bath and Body line up,
which includes the luscious
Kisses By Candlelight Body Soak.
Every gloss! Every glow! Just once,
you want it all.

Most Likely the Trumpet of the Lord Won't Sound Tonight

so you might as well cook
your Hamburger Helper,
break open a package of frozen peas,
turn off the TV,
put on some Ray Charles.
Make a pot of coffee.
Take out the trash.
Clean up that fur-ball throw-up stain.
Return those overdue library books,
pay the late fee.
Pick up a loaf of bread,
lunchmeat and an onion.
Build a fire.
Walk the dog.
Worm the cat.
Pluck your eyebrows.
Call your aunt in Indiana,
and your aunt in Arkansas.
Tell them it's raining here in Oregon,
and we're all doing just fine.

IV

Painting My Ceiling I Think of God

I have lost my roller pole extension.
My right arm and hand are numb,
so I've switched to my left hand.
The one chair I didn't take time to cover,
my hair, my face and eyelids, all paint-splattered.
Stiff-necked, dry-mouthed, weak-kneed,
rolling over what I've already rolled, waiting
for the blood to return to my strong arm,
half-blind and asphyxiated, here I stand, praying
there's enough paint left in the can
to finish this job.

Waiting

I am in the pediatric ward, of all places, with my Uncle Eugene
who's asleep with Demerol or morphine, his old blue glass eye
that terrified me as a child, staring straight at me. I'm sitting
at the end of his hospital bed in a padded, but uncomfortable
mauve-colored, straight-backed chair. My Auntie and my cousins
are taking a break for coffee and the chicken fried steak special
down at the cafeteria. I am thinking my uncle is lucky
to be stuck in pediatrics, because no babies have been born
and we have the place all to ourselves, unlike
his buddy, my father, who spent a week in the psycho ward
full of desperate moaning, waiting
to have his leg amputated.

It's that quiet moment we are sometimes given
with a beloved relative whose second stroke
has left him speechless, unable to swallow. I hear
the soft rattle of pneumonia in his breast.
Uncle's lips are swollen, crooked, smeared with Vaseline.
I think he looks handsome.
That's what I think.
I say, Will you look at this, Uncle?
This mauve stripe on my shirt exactly matches the color of this chair.
Leave it to me to be color-coordinated at a time like this.
That's what I say.

Ways to Die

Because you'd just as soon pass
up the bile, jaundice, screams, horror,
humiliation and helplessness of the cervical
and lung cancers that took their own sweet time
killing your mother and sister, you pray that you might
be the first in your family to die in your sleep, preferably
from old age. Surely it's okay to ask God to make it as painless
as possible, should both your legs be amputated, like your father's.

After all, two of your aunts who died from diabetic complications
had only toes removed, and got to wear their pink slippers up until
their last breaths. And what about your grandfather? One fatal heart attack.
No bypasses, diet changes or prescriptions. No nursing home, no home care.
Maybe you could ask for the cloudy-blue, but all-knowing stare that your
    uncle gave
after his last stroke. Or like your other uncle, just the soft swoosh through air
    as you fall off a roof.

Prayer, One

Bless our obsessive-compulsives,
our controlling extremist with ADD,
our manic, our low-grade depressed
who refuse Ritalin, Paxel, Prozac,
and even Saint John's Wort.
Bless our smokers, drinkers, our hooked-
on-Internet-porn addict. Bless our lazy
gossips, our hyperactive busybody,
our dyslexics, our slow one, our gay
one, and our autistic one. Bless our weary
souls, dysfunctional ways, our great big hearts.
Bless us Lord and keep us on the back pew
where we belong.

Prayer, Two

Bless those about to die
from complications of adult onset, type 2 diabetes,
who for countless years have stuck to their mini meals,
tasting banana cream pie and Oh Henry bars only in their dreams.
Comfort them as they wake up every hour on the hour to pee,
as they've long ago given up sweet iced tea, root beer, beer,
and all Coca-Colas. For goodness sake it's Christmas time,
and here I stand baking snickerdoodles, gingerbread men,
pecan and mincemeat pies, drinking hot spiced cider. God,
those blue bruises on their bellies and thighs, their night sweats,
psoriasis, neuropathy and dementia. Lord please bless
my sister, the way she forgets her own name
when her blood sugar shoots up over 400 on evenings
when she calls me higher than a kite, not sure of anything
but your grace and the promise of paradise.

Someone

There's the nephew planning
to stop drinking for thirty days,
because the uncle with the DUI
is living in his shed
until the attorney can get him off
with a fine, and ten days in jail.
There is the aunt with a broken heart and hip,
another aunt with a broken hip and pneumonia
who can't help thinking
about her recently departed third husband,
beloved Uncle Frank.
Oh all the uncles, all gone now!
Eugene, Ed, Ray, Hale, and Lee!
Oh Uncle Dennis
who we never even got to meet.
Oh the skinny, divorced sister
with a fibroid tumor,
hoping she doesn't look
as pregnant as she feels,
hoping she'll qualify for health care,
thankful for Section 8,
thankful the whole damn family's offered
to help her move into the tiny triplex—
even the diabetic sister
with major mood swings,
the cranky, recovering-from-bursitis sister,
the sister who's raising the granddaughter
who ran away again last night,

and the brother-in-law
who's happy to loan his truck
as soon as he returns from visiting
the bloated, yellow-eyed friend
stuck in stinky old Saint Catherine's,
whose only hope is a liver transplant—
if he stays off the sauce for six months.
Every time we turn around, someone's
checking out, moving out, in, or on,
or just stopping by, looking for someone else.
Someone with a box of doughnuts,
hoping coffee's on. Someone fired,
someone promoted, someone praising God,
ready to be baptized. Someone high,
someone lonely, someone drunk,
someone low.

Godspeed

Blessed be the man who finally buys the used car of his dreams,
the man who married my sister and took on our entire family's needs,
the man who always gives a portion to the Lord, helps orphans
in Russia, missionaries in Africa, and sisters-in-law on welfare.
Blessed be the man with a degree from Cal Berkeley
who knows big words, but doesn't use them. Blessed be

the man who waits until his cancer's in remission,
and his hip replacement's healing nicely. Blessed be the man who waits
until his modest home is paid for, his wife's future secure.

God bless the patriot-red body lines, the soft gray leather bucket seats,
the low-mileage 350 with four-on-the-floor 1993 Trans Am. Godspeed,
buddy.

Small

I have always been
the youngest, smallest sister.
The hip-less, thigh-less, breast-less recipient
of countless hand-me-downs, which never fit.
Little Ginger. Little quiet, shy, skinny, sick with pneumonia,
scared of her own shadow baby of the family.

My middle sister is gone now. Cancer.
I am wearing one of her coats, a soft, lightweight yellow jacket
that almost fits. Yellow is not my color. I think of her every time I wear it.
I am also wearing my oldest sister's first husband's dead aunt's bra. 34 B.
Underwire. A perfect fit. There were five of them, like new, in the box
of her clothes that her sister gave to my sister, knowing
some of Imogene's clothes might fit that youngest Dearstine girl.

I am the youngest, smallest sister. Lucky me.

How to Talk about Jesus

It's easy to tell your sister she's got a black thing
in the corner of her eye, some mascara, a little bug,
maybe an eyelash or something. It's not quite as easy
to tell her she's got a booger hanging. Nobody likes
to mention boogers. If you're driving down the road,
you can dig Kleenex out of your purse, say, Hon,
you got a booger. She'll maybe ask, Which nose hole?
You'll tell her. She'll get it with the Kleenex you offered,
check in the rearview to make sure, and on you'll go
to work, wherever. But how about a stranger, a pretty lady
in the grocery line with pink lipstick on her front teeth
as she smiles, offering to let you go ahead
because you only have a loaf of French bread?
I once pointed a finger toward my next door neighbor's crotch
when we were talking at our mailboxes.
Two big green praying mantises were mating
right there on his button fly. We laughed. I really don't
know how to throw Shadrach, Meshach or Abednego
into a casual chat with my pharmacist about the weather,
but I've learned it's best to talk apples before Eve,
to start with little things.

After Church

Cruising down Hwy 38, going to visit our brother,
my sisters and I get into a serious religious discussion.
I am the youngest sister, but the oldest Christian.
I get a little loud, according to my back seat sister
who's having a diabetic low, so we stop for orange juice,
maple bars and coffee. Back on the road, I apologize,
only to get wound up again over whether or not
Revelation's thousand-year reign is literal.
I raise my hands to make a point, spilling hot coffee
down the front of my blouse and all over my new khaki Dockers.
I laugh till I cry. My behind-the-wheel sister, also crying,
says she had a dream the other night that Osama Bin Laden
was holding a gun to her head, asking if she was a Christian.
My back seat sister slaps the back of my seat. She's sorry,
but she has to go to the bathroom. She's also sorry
for volunteering to sit in back where she hears only half
of what we're saying, and can't see anything
but the backs of our pointed little heads.

Guilty

It happens
to be a beautiful morning,
the orange sun huge,
slanting through the valley fog
all the way to the county courthouse
where my brother pleads guilty
to driving under the influence,
is handcuffed,
sentenced to ten days in jail,
thirty months probation,
a fifteen hundred dollar fine,
to be paid in fifty dollar per month
installments, all as we expected.
No slack for repeat offenders,
even a kind fifty-seven year-old
clean-cut handsome man
whose last arrest was six long years ago,
after our father, and then our sister died.
A man with children in another county
who are used to their dad serving them
hot oatmeal and buttered toast
every morning before school. My brother
nods his head toward me in thanks, I guess,
for the ride here, as he follows
fellow jail mates, single file
down the long hall.

Recovering from a Bout of Bursitis,

thrilled to finally be able to sleep
on the not-so-inflamed shoulder, to do that
turn-in-the-middle-of-the-night-turn,
to roll with a dream, side to side,
or just flip flop around because you can.
You can button your pants, hook your bra,
shower and shave under both arms,
tie your shoes, gather up your hair
in your left hand, before you brush your teeth.
You can take off one blouse, put on another.
Open your arms wide, fold towels and sheets,
make your bed like a pro. You can drive
with either hand, or both!
You can just stand around flapping
your arms like an idiot, or an angel.
You can thank God for the new old you,
set new goals, rededicate, commit,
confess your sins. You've been meaning to
volunteer in a soup line, clean out
your old, arthritic neighbor's gutters.
You can hug anyone, anytime,
for any reason, you could change
your whole life if you wanted to.

Late Walk

I pass up a pine cone
a cigarette butt
and a pop top
for three little sticks
all about the same size
all brown and not
particularly pretty.
Three twigs. Three little
skinny, regular brown twigs.
I name them all Twiggy.
I roll them between
my thumb and forefinger
and some bark falls off.
I hold them
up to my nose and sniff.
They have no smell,
but then again
I have a sinus infection.
I lay the Twiggies
in the palm of my hand,
close my fingers around them,
put them in my coat pocket,
head on home to chicken soup,
garlic bread and Sudafed.
I consider going back
for the pop top. God,
wouldn't that be stupid.

Yes

Have you ever found yourself
standing, say, in your hallway
with one hand on your hip, a little
frown between your eyes?
Maybe you're looking
for your Bible, your car keys, the red
belt that matches your red slacks.
But you are just standing there.
Maybe you are tired,
got troubles on your mind,
dry patches on your face, a little
pain in your heart. You are cold.
You are hot. You're not sure
what day it is, but know you need
to be getting ready to go
to the store, to the cleaners,
to church or somewhere.
Maybe you are singing
an old Jethro Tull song, *well it's Bungle*
in the Jungle, and that's all right by me.
Oh yeah yeah yeah, and you don't
remember the rest of the words
so you just repeat the chorus
over and over, wondering how
in the world, in the middle of
everything, you stop to sing
a song you haven't heard in twenty years—
not even your favorite Tull tune—

why not *Aqualung,* why not
I Left My Heart In San Francisco,
or *Amazing Grace*—there's
a good old hymn, sung at every funeral
you've ever attended. It's been four years
since your sister died, your children
are grown, have good jobs and health insurance,
your husband's at work, it's raining hard,
the river's rising. You need
to bring in wood for the fire.
You need to pray and sing *Yes,*
Jesus loves me.

Old Cleaning Ladies

We find ourselves
reaching for paper towels
in public restrooms,
buffing little sections
of sink, tile, toilet or wall.
It's not a matter
of caring about dirt
or germs, it's not
a matter of pride.

Without thinking
we look under counters
for a toilet brush,
cleansers—Comet, Windex,
409, Fantastik, anything
to make something
shine.

"May the favor of the Lord our God rest upon us;
establish the work of our hands for us—
yes, establish the work of our hands."
—Psalm 90:17